Dear Me

Poems of loss, grief, and hope
in New York's darkest days

STEPHANIE SLOANE

the three
tomatoes
The Three Tomatoes Book Publishing

Published 2020 Printed in the United States of America

ISBN: 978-0-578-72204-7

Library of Congress Control Number: 2020912127

For information address:

The Three Tomatoes Book Publishing

6 Soundview Rd. Glen Cove, NY 11542

Cover and interior images: Stephanie Sloane

Cover design: Susan Herbst

All company and/or product names may be trade names, logos, trademarks, and/or registered trademarks and are the property of their respective owners.

Dear Me

Poems of loss, grief, and hope
in New York's darkest days

Dedication

for Mike

May 1, 2020

What I Learned During Lockdown

Knowing it's going to be bad and being bad
Are two different things
How does one heal from the loss of a spouse?
By moving forward
Impossible when movement is not permitted
Not in any direction
Everyone says I'm strong
Am I?

Dear Me

May 2, 2020

The Good Old Days

O for the good old days
When all we had to do was show up!

Stephanie Sloane

May 3, 2020

Do I Need a Therapist?

I think I'm ok
What can a therapist tell me
That I don't already know?

Dear Me

Stephanie Sloane

May 4, 2020

Pretty Prison
————————

If someone had told me
Just a few months ago
That I, a native New Yorker,
Would come to hate New York City,
I wouldn't have believed them
Yet here I am now
In this pretty prison

Dear Me

May 5, 2020

The World Has Become a Scary Place
— —

We have become unmoored
We have only questions, no answers
We can't make any plans
We have no idea of the future
Or even, at our ages, if there is one

Stephanie Sloane

May 6, 2020

A Friendly Face

I'd do anything to see a friendly face
Or any face
How long can we subsist
With only telephone contact?

Dear Me

Stephanie Sloane

May 7, 2020

Abandonment

New York on lockdown
Apartment dwellers with second homes
Abandon their city abodes
For points north and east
Leaving the rest of us
With views of empty apartments
Drawn shades
Half-empty buildings
Desolate streets

Dear Me

May 8, 2020

Dinner Delivered
– – – – – – – – – –

When our lives are limited
Small things become important
Like the food we eat
An email from the independent grocer
Offers stuffed cabbage, my favorite
Too much temptation to resist
It tastes just like my grandmother's
I didn't know golden raisins still exist

Stephanie Sloane

May 9, 2020

Don't Touch
— — — — — — — —

What are the long-term implications
Of not being able to touch another human being?
Babies who are denied being held,
Nuzzled and touched can even die
Isn't touching a natural instinct?
What will happen to us?
Is there a repository somewhere
Where former touch and being touched
Can be saved?

Dear Me

Stephanie Sloane

May 10, 2020

The First of Everything is Hard

My first Mother's Day alone brings
That feeling of relief when another day ends
Family Zoom gathering without content
Because life now has no content

Dear Me

May 11, 2020

Forever
— — — — —

I hadn't considered what was ahead
I thought our lives would go on forever
As they were
Perhaps foolishness
Perhaps survival

Stephanie Sloane

May 12, 2020

Shelter in Place
————————

I can't go outside
Well, technically, I can
But TV ads say Stay Home
On many daily phone calls
I learn some peers take daily walks
Is it safe?
What keeps me inside?
Fear

Dear Me

May 13, 2020

What I Look Forward To

A bell rings and I find
A mystery package outside my door
Sometimes it's food
Sometimes laundry
Sometimes a combination of goodies
That don't go together
A book, underpants, emery boards
All in the same box
Left outside my door
By mysterious strangers
Whose faces I never see

Stephanie Sloane

When the package makes it inside,
There it sits for its second life
24 hours for cardboard
3 hours for paper
2 days for cloth

A junkyard of assorted mismatched items
That felt essential when they were ordered

Dear Me

Dear Me

May 14, 2020

Zoom or Facetime?
— — — — — — — — — — — —

We can only see each other
On computer screens
By arrangement

Stephanie Sloane

May 15, 2020

We Have Too Much Time on Our Hands

Whoever thought that my friends and I
Who usually discuss life
Would devote so much time to discussing
What TV shows we should watch?

Dear Me

May 16, 2020

Just for A Moment

I time my dinners
Towards the end of each meal
Precisely at 7
A wonderful sound rises from the street
Apartment dwellers and passers-by alike
Celebrate first responders, essential workers
People on balconies bang pans,
Walkers clap, horns honk
Just for a moment, it's my city again

Dear Me

May 17, 2020

A Spring Day

I couldn't resist venturing outside
Armed with mask and gloves
Sunglasses too, since I learned
The virus can enter your eyes,
I met a friend in Central Park
The park was beautiful as ever
Even with everything closed
But meeting a friend was the best
I have friends and family here
I just can't see them

Dear Me

May 18, 2020

At 7 PM

Inspired by street sounds louder than usual
Encouraged by an open window across the street
I opened mine and had my first bang-on-a-pan
It only lasted a minute, but it felt good

Stephanie Sloane

Dear Me

May 19, 2020

Lack of Concentration

I can't write
I can't read
I can't draw
I can't knit

But maybe I can fix up an old house

I can move back to where I belong
Where I have friends
Where I'll have family
Where I belong

Stephanie Sloane

May 20, 2020

It's All New

I opened my first bottle of Prosecco tonight
For myself
It wasn't difficult
Just something my husband always did
Have no idea why
It's not a particularly masculine or feminine activity
Why is it different from opening wine?
Never thought about it before
Just another thing to get used to

Dear Me

May 21, 2020

I'm Not Married

Just realized I'm not married
How can that be?
I've been married for most of my life
I don't know how to be single
Or a widow
Why don't I feel different?

Stephanie Sloane

Dear Me

May 22, 2020

Shopping After Two Months

My first trip to a supermarket
Familiar and unfamiliar at the same time
So, this is where all the items are
Those things marked unavailable online
Toilet paper, waffles, cooking spray
All beckoning
But wait
As I avoid other shoppers,
Keeping social distance
They avoid me too
Acting as if they're afraid of me

May 23, 2020

So Many Widows

So many widows
Kindly offer to speak with me
They've been there.
I want to call them
To learn from their experience
But I can't seem to do so

Dear Me

May 24, 2020

We're All Mourning

We're mourning the lives we had
And didn't appreciate until they were gone
The freedom to come and go as we pleased
Will it ever return?
Nobody knows for sure

Dear Me

May 25, 2020

Today's Paper

After a temporary suspension,
My newspaper delivery has resumed
One of today's many headlines asks
"Can Coney Island Survive This?"
Can we?

Stephanie Sloane

May 26, 2020

The Visit
— — — — —

An uplifting day
Returning to where I used to feel at peace
Finding I still do

Dear Me

May 27, 2020

A New Life
— — — — — — —

Is it possible that I've managed to design
A new life for myself?
I loved the old one
I would wake up each morning and think
What do I want to do today?
The possibilities were endless
All of them good

Dear Me

May 28, 2020

The Secret

Perhaps I've discovered the secret
It's not that I can't burst into tears
At a moment's notice
It's not that at the moment of waking
I don't expect to see him there
But all my waking moments are not sad
I've found a new focus
One that gives me and others
Something to look forward to

Dear Me

May 29, 2020

Good vs. Bad
— — — — — — —

The bad memories of those last few months are
fading
Replacing them are the good
Trips, vacations, celebrations, parties,
Warm dinners with friends, family get togethers

But some will never fade
Like a Zoom funeral that many couldn't join
Like an urn that I can't bring home
Like boxes of photos that I can't view

When life returns to somewhat normal
There will be a Memorial
Will that be a good thing?
Maybe…

Stephanie Sloane

May 30, 2020

What I'm Getting Used To

Living in an apartment meant for us both
In a neighborhood we would explore together
Cooking for one, dining alone
Endless pandemic days
Can walking the hall to the incinerator room
Masked and gloved
Really be the highlight of my day?

Dear Me

May 31, 2020

Time to Exercise
— — — — — — — — —

Sounds simple
But is it?
So many choices
Online classes offer
Yoga, Pilates, Gentle Pilates,
Stretching, Feldenkrais, Reiki
Maybe tomorrow

June 1, 2020

Last Night I Cried

Unlike before, it was not for personal loss
But for what is happening to my country
Demonstrations in cities
Fires, looting, violence
Protestors angry, shouting
Shattering glass
Shattering lives

Dear Me

Stephanie Sloane

June 2, 2020

Lockdown Squared

A curfew that began at 11PM
Has painted the streets empty
From my window, the city that never sleeps
Is asleep
As if it didn't look enough like a ghost town before
With so few people and cars
Now it is complete
With none

Dear Me

Stephanie Sloane

June 3, 2020

Curfew
————

Sirens and police cars below
Helicopters above
Where am I?
This doesn't feel like New York
Or even like the United States
It feels like a war-torn country
Only instead of hiding in a bunker
I'm confined to a luxury apartment
Does It really matter?
The feelings must be the same

Dear Me

Stephanie Sloane

June 4, 2020

Protest
— — — —

Strange quietude calls to me
I open my window
For an unexpected surprise
Marchers chant "Black Lives Matter"
As they pass
An orderly masked parade
They wave to those of us who watch
And I return their waves

Dear Me

Stephanie Sloane

June 5, 2020

Things Change

The rare times I emerge from my apartment
I usually walk east
Past stores and restaurants
All closed
On occasion I head west
Past boutiques, galleries, museums
All closed
What a shock to now see
Madison Avenue
Once elegant
All boarded up

Dear Me

Stephanie Sloane

June 6, 2020

This Is What It's Come To

Another outing
After another nine days indoors
Meeting a friend in the street
With nowhere to go
Settling at a bus stop bench
Trying to stay six feet apart
While signaling the empty buses that approach
Don't stop here

Dear Me

Stephanie Sloane

June 7, 2020

Grasp Life Now
— — — — — — — —

The gods of loss decry
Wait one year after loss
To make major decisions

But life is too short
So, that year condenses to months
I can stave off the loneliness
By providing a loving place
To be with family and friends
Now, while there's still time

Dear Me

June 8, 2020

Phase I
— — — —

Today, the lockdown is officially over
After one hundred days
How will that change our lives?
It has already changed mine
It has forced me to figure out
How I want to live the rest of my life
Happily

Dear Me

Acknowledgments

My deepest thanks to all my friends and family for your loving support when I needed it most.

About the Author

A native New Yorker, born and raised in the Bronx, who now lives in Manhattan, Stephanie Sloane has had an eclectic career encompassing many creative endeavors. With a BA in Fine Art and Theatre, and an MS in Education and Art, she started out teaching art and dance. She has acted in commercials, off-off Broadway theater, and in films. As activities coordinator of a psychiatric unit for eleven years, she initiated a program that included art and dance therapies. She went on to become an art dealer and for seventeen years was associate director of

Pace Prints. She has written two plays, "Toujours L'Amour" which was staged in NYC last year, and "Bronx Light/Bronx Dark." She enjoys cooking, knitting, drawing, jewelry-making, moving and decorating.

She was married for fifty-eight years to her husband, Michael, who recently passed away. They raised three children, Todd, Gregg and Danielle, while living in Suffern, New York. She has eight grandchildren. The loss of her husband at the same time as the pandemic prompted her to write her first, but not her last, book of poetry with photographs.

Dear Me

CPSIA information can be obtained
at www.ICGtesting.com
Printed in the USA
BVHW021800300820
587657BV00021B/1306